Easy Flute Solos

with Piano Accompaniment

Order No. AM 40320
International Standard Book Number: 0.8256.12083.X

Exclusive Distributors:
Music Sales Corporation
225 Park Avenue South, New York, NY 10003
Music Sales Limited
8/9 Frith Street, London W1V 5TZ England
Music Sales Pty. Limited
120 Rothschild Street, Rosebery, Sydney, NSW 2018, Australia

Printed in the United States of America by
Vicks Lithograph and Printing Corporation

Amsco Publications
New York/London/Sydney

TITLE INDEX

COMPOSER INDEX

Cockles And Mussels
(MOLLY MALONE)

Old Irish Song

When Love Is Kind

Old English Song

A Capital Ship

Old English Folk Song

Grandfather's Clock

HENRY C. WORK

Twinkle, Twinkle, Little Star

Children's Song

Kingdom Coming

HENRY C. WORK

There's Music In The Air

GEORGE F. ROOT

That Big Rock Candy Mountain

American Song

Hand Me Down My Walking Cane

American Song

Bonny Eloise

J. R. THOMAS

Wait For The Wagon

R. B. BUCKLEY

John Peel

Old English Hunting Song

Where Did You Get That Hat?

JOSEPH J. SULLIVAN

Laura Lee

STEPHEN FOSTER

Some Folks

STEPHEN FOSTER

Jenny June

STEPHEN FOSTER

Old Dog Tray

STEPHEN FOSTER

De Camptown Races

STEPHEN FOSTER

Nelly Bly

STEPHEN FOSTER

The Glendy Burk

STEPHEN FOSTER

Katy Bell

STEPHEN FOSTER

Short'nin' Bread

U. S. Folk Song

Oh! Dem Golden Slippers

U. S. Spiritual

She'll Be Comin' 'Round The Mountain

U.S. Folk Song

Shoo Fly, Don't Bother Me

U.S. Folk Song

Deep River

U. S. Spiritual

Go Down, Moses

U. S. Spiritual

Nobody Knows The Trouble I've Seen

U. S. Spiritual

Roll, Jordan, Roll

U. S. Spiritual

Swing Low, Sweet Chariot

U. S. Spiritual

Somebody's Knocking At Your Door

U. S. Spiritual

All Through The Night

Welsh Folk Song

Oh, Dear, What Can The Matter Be?

Old English Song

Roaming

Gypsy Song

Juanita

Spanish Melody

I've A Longing
In My Heart For You, Louise

CHAS. K. HARRIS

White Wings

BANKS WINTER

Flow Gently, Sweet Afton

J. E. SPILMAN

Jingle Bells

J. PIERPONT

Darling Nelly Gray

B. R. HANBY

In The Sweet By And By

J. P. WEBSTER

There Is A Tavern In The Town

English Folk Song

Dreaming

J. ANTON DAILEY

O Canada
(CANADIAN ANTHEM)

C. LAVALLEE
& R. S. WEIR

The Maple Leaf Forever
(CANADIAN ANTHEM)

ALEXANDER MUIR

Come To The Sea!
(VIENI SUL MAR)

Venetian Melody

Peri Waltzes

CHAS. D'ALBERT

The Black Hawk Waltz

MARY E. WALSH

Star Of The East
(CHRISTMAS BALLAD)

A. KENNEDY

Ave Verum Corpus

WOLFGANG MOZART

Ashley Polka

Old Dance Tune

Martha Polka

Old Dance Tune

Jenny Lind Polka

Old Dance Tune

The Thunderer
MARCH

JOHN PHILIP SOUSA

Picadore March

JOHN PHILIP SOUSA

The National Fencibles

MARCH

JOHN PHILIP SOUSA

The Loyal Legion
MARCH

JOHN PHILIP SOUSA

The High School Cadets
MARCH

JOHN PHILIP SOUSA

The Gladiators
MARCH

JOHN PHILIP SOUSA